T0120574

HOPE FOR YOUR CANCER JOURNEY

A FIRST STEP IN THE JOURNEY

Ruth Phillips, RN, BSN, MS, OCN

WESTBOW
PRESS®
A DIVISION OF THOMAS NELSON
& ZONDERVAN

Copyright © 2021 Ruth Phillips, RN, BSN, MS, OCN.

All rights reserved. No part of this book may be used or reproduced by any means, graphic, electronic, or mechanical, including photocopying, recording, taping or by any information storage retrieval system without the written permission of the author except in the case of brief quotations embodied in critical articles and reviews.

This book is a work of non-fiction. Unless otherwise noted, the author and the publisher make no explicit guarantees as to the accuracy of the information contained in this book and in some cases, names of people and places have been altered to protect their privacy.

WestBow Press books may be ordered through booksellers or by contacting:

WestBow Press
A Division of Thomas Nelson & Zondervan
1663 Liberty Drive
Bloomington, IN 47403
www.westbowpress.com
844-714-3454

Because of the dynamic nature of the Internet, any web addresses or links contained in this book may have changed since publication and may no longer be valid. The views expressed in this work are solely those of the author and do not necessarily reflect the views of the publisher, and the publisher hereby disclaims any responsibility for them.

Any people depicted in stock imagery provided by Getty Images are models, and such images are being used for illustrative purposes only. Certain stock imagery © Getty Images.

Scripture quotations taken from The Holy Bible, New International Version® NIV® Copyright © 1973 1978 1984 2011 by Biblica, Inc. TM. Used by permission. All rights reserved worldwide.

ISBN: 978-1-6642-2749-1 (sc)
ISBN: 978-1-6642-2748-4 (hc)
ISBN: 978-1-6642-2750-7 (e)

Library of Congress Control Number: 2021905320

Print information available on the last page.

WestBow Press rev. date: 03/31/2021

This book is a compilation of years spent caring for cancer patients and is dedicated to all those whom I have had the privilege and joy to care for.

I would also like to thank Wayne Miller, Carol Gray, Rachelle Smith, and my three boys, Hayden, Peyton, and Keegan, for their support and encouragement. It has been an exciting journey that we all pray will be a blessing to those in need.

CONTENTS

INTRODUCTION

Hope for Your Cancer Journey is a compilation of resources, personal health care experiences, and anecdotes designed to empower individuals facing a cancer diagnosis. Cancer is challenging. No two people experience the same situation on this path. It is important not to compare yourself to others. Follow your heart when making decisions, knowing that you know you better than anyone. This book aims to provide the confidence you need to make decisions about your care.

There are many opportunities to take control. Our goal is for you to find guidance within these pages. Do not feel obligated to read each page or even read this book from beginning to end. Find the chapters that address your current situation and start there. Share other chapters with loved ones who may be willing to dig deeper and take steps to support you in reaching out to resources or in planning for you. Our hope is to empower each of you to live full and active lives to the best of your abilities. We hope by sharing hints and tips, you will be successful in achieving your goals.

Cancer is a daily journey. Just as no two individuals will experience cancer the same way, no two days on this journey will be the same. Some days will be filled with joy, others with anxiety or a feeling of being overwhelmed, and many will leave you feeling tired from long hours of treatments. The suggestions supplied can keep the joyful memories alive longer and reduce the frequency of those moments that seem overwhelming. Seek the support and resources that will make life easier and more enjoyable while managing your cancer diagnosis.

CHAPTER 1

CANCER CANNOT CHANGE THE PLANS GOD HAS FOR YOU

One of the first questions many cancer patients ask is "Why me?" Unfortunately, the answers to these questions are not always easy to come by. What I do know is that regardless of why, you can have hope. Hope is a part of healing, so I feel it's important to start our journey together here. Psalm 107:29 (NIV) says, "He stilled the storm to a whisper; the waves of the sea were hushed." A diagnosis of cancer can leave you feeling as though you are in the middle of a storm. Hope can be found in believing that God will help calm the storm within and around you. Cancer cannot change the plans God has for you. "'For I know the plans I have for you,' declares the Lord, 'plans to prosper you and not to harm you, plans to give you hope and a future'" (Jeremiah 29:11 NIV).

Even though *Grit* by Angela Duckworth isn't about overcoming cancer, it does speak to overcoming obstacles. A diagnosis of cancer can be a huge obstacle to individuals and their family and friends. So, how do we overcome an obstacle such as cancer? Hope is one part of that process. Hope, according to Angela Duckworth, can have two paths: one that assumes the universe will solve a problem and one that assumes finding control over a problem will lead to a solution[1]. I believe the second path to hope provides the most

---

[1] Angela Duckworth, *Grit* (London: Vermilion, 2019).

amazing results. This path includes learning more about a diagnosis, a traditional cancer treatment, or even a complementary treatment. It is the hope needed for those dealing with cancer.

I relate this type of hope to empowerment. It may mean we need to change our inner voices through prayer, positive thoughts, meditation, and/or visualization. Talking through our struggles privately with God or with someone else willing to listen can lighten the load we are carrying and even bring clarity when we are not expecting it. Sometimes finding this level of control over your cancer may mean that you need to ask for help, and that is OK too. Friends and family want to help. Depend on the Lord for the power to take one step at a time, and trust one breath at a time. He will help you figure out the part of His plan that you are to discover and will bring hope. Isaiah 40:31 (NIV) reminds us that "those who hope in the LORD will renew their strength. They will soar on wings like eagles; they will run and not grow weary; they will walk and not be faint."

As I have been writing this book, Alex Trebek passed away after living with pancreatic cancer for seven months. A friend shared her thoughts on his example, which I feel is important to pass on. Mona's focus is on leadership, but Alex is a wonderful example for individuals with cancer as well. I have added a thought called "cancer connection" to each of Mona's thoughts to highlight how Alex Trebek's example can benefit you.

What Am I Learning from *Jeopardy* Host Alex Trebek That's Deepening My Understanding of Leadership? [2]

By Mona DelSole

I am seeing an impactful leader who has not missed a day of work since

---

[2] Mona DelSole, "Alex Trebec's Courageous Leadership," November 9, 2020, https://www.linkedin.com/pulse/alex-trebecs-courageous-leadership-mona-delsole-mpa/.

being diagnosed and shares his personal battle with positivity and for millions to witness. While I am not much of a game show follower, what I do know is that it is hard enough to be an impactful leader under the best of circumstances. Add to this cancer, chemotherapy, and all the symptoms associated with it, Alex Trebek takes his platform to the next level. I see him as an inspirational model of self-leadership. His story grabs my attention.

Here are characteristics of Alex Trebek's leadership:

- Connection: Alex connects with contestants and audiences of all ages while sharing the details of his battle. His intergenerational communication skills are personal, genuine, and open. Alex helps contestants become the star of the show by asking questions and actively listening. And when he is speaking to his audience, those same skills help him connect, inspire, and build relationships that contribute to the outpouring of support he receives today.

Cancer connection: Relationships are an important part of managing the ups and downs of a cancer diagnosis. Be open with loved ones about your needs and your fears. Allow them to support you.

- Authenticity: Alex openly talks about dealing with depression, his lost energy, and more and gets teary-eyed when talking to his audience. But he states, "I don't even bother to explain it anymore, I just experience it. I know it's part of who I am, and I keep going."

Cancer connection: Expect setbacks on your journey. Embrace them and keep going. Stay positive.

- Courage: While this seems like one of the most obvious leadership traits coming through, being on a national platform adds another level of courage. It certainly takes courage to face this diagnosis in your quietest moments. It takes even more courage to be transparent, humble, and vulnerable when sharing on a national platform. I can't help but think his example of self-leadership will impact many. Courage—not just in what he is personally battling but in his decision to be real and authentic with so many.

Cancer connection: Every day, there will be challenges—changes, unknowns, and struggles—some days more than others. Whatever it brings, you can choose to face it with courage, hope, and a positive mindset.

CHAPTER 2

CANCER AND THE LATEST ADVANCEMENTS IN ONCOLOGY

Cancer treatments and even the tests used to diagnose cancer have changed dramatically over the last twenty years. Keeping up to date on the latest thinking is challenging. This book does not hope to cover all that has changed, nor will it try to predict the future of oncology. As you face your diagnosis, ask questions about the latest treatments, opportunities to participate in clinical trials, or even if there is something new coming that would make a difference in your care. I highly recommend looking at opportunities for clinical trials. Many people miss these opportunities as a result of fear and a lack of understanding. Clinical trials are extremely safe and at the minimum will provide you with results that are at least the same as the standard of care. As with all treatments, be sure to talk with your provider and ask questions.

Forbes published an article back on June 10, 2015, that highlights the positive steps that have been taken in combatting cancer. Some of these highlights include the use of immunotherapies, which activate the body's immune system to attack cancer cells. These immunotherapies are being used across many cancer types as well as in combination with other drugs to improve the outcomes of cancer patients[3]. *Forbes* also

---

[3] Howard Gleckman, "Big Strides in Cancer Treatment Will Increase Long-Term Care Needs," *Forbes*, June 10, 2015, https://www.forbes.com/sites/howardgleckman/2015/06/10/big-strides-in-cancer-treatment-will-increase-long-term-care-needs/?sh=d85050c627be.

highlighted our ability to sequence genes quickly and cost-effectively. This is an exciting aspect of cancer care. The ability to understand a cancer's genetic makeup is changing how oncologists look at and treat cancer. As a result, targeted drug therapies have been developed to alter the way an abnormal gene works, ultimately stopping a cancer from continuing to grow. If your oncologist has not mentioned genetic testing of your cancer, it may be worth asking about. The National Cancer Institute is trying to determine if gene mutations that are found in a particular type of cancer behave the same way in other cancers. Having this information may change much of how we treat cancer in the future. Other researchers are looking at ways to use immune cells that have been modified to carry medication to a target on a cancer cell. They have also found ways to use viruses to stimulate the immune system to attack cancer cells.

There is so much to be hopeful for. Tomorrow may hold the treatment or cure you are searching for.

Nutritional oncology is now more accepted among traditional medicine and often is part of the plan of care for patients. Nutritional oncology looks at how our diets impact both the development of cancer and other diseases, as well as how diet can help us combat cancer. NIH-funded research is now being undertaken to understand the impact of diet on cancer. Dr. Li of the Angiogenesis Foundation examined "the role that food and their extracts can play in the disruption of new blood vessel development in solid tumors.[4]" He believes the results you can get by eating the proper foods can be "similar to or are more potent than some pharmaceuticals, including anticancer drugs.[4]" There is

---

[4] William W Li, "Keynote Presentation: Dietary Modification of the Tumor Microenvironment," quoted in "Angiogenesis and Nutritional Oncology: New Frontiers in the Approach to Cancer Therapy," *CCA News* 1, no. 2 (October 2020).

still a lot more research to be done to prove this, but it is a step in the right direction.

Dr. Li, like many others, believes God designed our bodies to protect and heal themselves. He outlined the three aspects of our immune systems that are important in the fight against cancer and in the understanding of how tumors develop and grow. These include the following:

1. Angiogenesis: Angiogenesis is the normal process responsible for the creation of new blood vessels from existing blood vessels. Cancer uses this process to allow more nutrients to be taken in by the cancer cells, which, in turn, helps them survive. Phytoestrogens, found in soy and lycopene and tomatoes and citrus fruits, have been shown to stop angiogenesis.

2. Regeneration: Humans are able to create new tissue when healthy tissue is damaged. As we get older, this ability weakens, which is why we often see cancer in older adults. Diets that are high in fat, salt, and sugar can also reduce our ability to regenerate healthy cells. Some diets, such as the Mediterranean and Okinawan diets, calorie-restricted diets, and intermittent-fasting diets, have been shown to lead to improved healing in response to injury, illness, and surgery.

3. Microbiome and the immune system: The microbiome is made up of bacteria, fungi, viruses, and other microbes. In health care, we refer to the gut microbiota as an important part of our immune system. When the bacteria in our guts is healthy, typically so are we. Dr. Li emphasized that a healthy gut starts and ends with a healthy diet.

Another aspect of Nutritional Oncology is learning how to eat. Research is pointing to eating intuitively with success measured by improved health and wellness. To eat intuitively, you should eat only when hungry, stop eating when you are full or no longer hungry, and avoid restricting foods unless it is required for a medical condition. It is important to pay attention to your body and listen to the signals it is providing when practicing intuitive eating. More on diet can be found in chapter 6.

Technology is also being used to improve cancer care. Through early identification and management of side effects, individuals with cancer can remain on treatment at the medication doses that are prescribed. This has been shown to improve a cancer patient's survival. Ethan Basch reported a study looking at the value of a survey that was given to patients on a weekly basis to identify side effects from chemotherapy. The completed survey was sent to health care providers to review and to follow up with individuals who were having problems tolerating their cancer treatment. This weekly survey alone was able to improve the overall survival of patients in the study by seven months[5]. There are now companies developing digital health products to allow patients to report side effects in real time, and some will provide patients with suggestions on how to manage side effects that are not severe in nature. Even if you do not have access to these technologies at your oncologist's office, there is an important lesson to be learned. If you are experiencing any side effects, including depression or anxiety, talk to your doctor so he or she can provide the help you need. No side effect is too small or unimportant to share. It will make a big difference in the results of your care.

The technology that you have handy may also be

---

[5] Ethan Basch et al., "Symptom Monitoring With Patient-Reported Outcomes during Routine Cancer Treatment: A Randomized Controlled Trial," *Journal of Clinical Oncology* 34, no. 6 (February 2016): 557–565, https://doi.org/10.1200/jco.2015.63.0830.

valuable. Using the *alarm* feature on your phone may help with scheduling medications or appointments. You can also use the *notes* function to keep track of side effects or questions you may have for your physician. Smart devices around the home may be used to set reminders and can keep track of information you want to remember. While many digital health companies have yet to pair their devices with smart home devices, they are considering the use of this technology. The reason they have not yet done so is they are trying to figure out how to keep your data safe.

Many years ago, the World Health Organization said that it may be possible to overcome many of the world's greatest health issues without developing new medications, if we could find a way to ensure unhealthy individuals actually took the prescribed doses of medications they were given. Cancer care is no different. Many patients skip doses of medication because of side effects or the cost of the medication. Taking the proper dose of medication is important. Keep in mind if you are experiencing side effects, continuing treatment could possibly cause harm. For example, if you develop mouth sores from your treatment, continuing your treatment could cause the mouth sores to get worse and make it difficult for you to eat. In situations such as this, it is essential to speak with your doctor, as there are many things that can be done to resolve the side effect while continuing to fight your cancer. It is important to find a balance between not missing treatments and taking them when required. Be open and honest with your health care team. They are there to support you.

We have already turned many heart conditions into a manageable chronic disease. With stents, devices, and drugs, cardiac patients now live long, relatively normal lives. We have done this with some forms of breast cancer and even chronic myelogenous leukemia.

Life expectancy in the US is now at 79.8 years. As we continue to improve the ability to diagnosis cancer early and improve upon the treatments we are developing, we can have hope that life expectancy will continue to increase.

Technology includes the use of telehealth services, virtual reality, artificial intelligence, and so much more. Telehealth has been rapidly adopted as a result of COVID-19 and is seen as an addition to care already being provided. One of the most important goals of telehealth is ensuring all individuals have access to quality cancer care regardless of where they live. Telehealth has been shown to reduce hospitalizations by 38 percent, reduce readmissions by 31 percent, increase the likelihood of spending fewer days in the hospital by 63 percent, and increase patient engagement in care[6]. Ask your health

---

[6] Reena Pande et al., "Leveraging Remote Behavioral Health Interventions to Improve Medical Outcomes and Reduce Costs," *The American Journal of Managed Care* 21, no. 2 (February 2015).

care provider if they offer telehealth services. It may save a trip to the office while providing the support you need.

Virtual reality is another exciting new technology that is being used to help reduce anxiety and nausea and to help patients visualize their body attacking cancer cells. If your institution offers this technology, you may want to give it a try.

The Patient Empowerment Network developed the Digital Sherpa Program[7] to help patients and their families become technologically fluent. If you need assistance with the technology being offered at your institution, ask for help. Guide for Hope[8] provides cancer-coaching services covering a wide range of topics, including technology assistance.

[7] Andrea Connors, "Digital Sherpa™ Program," Patient Empowerment Network, July 23, 2020, https://powerfulpatients.org/digital-sherpa-program/.

[8] Ruth Phillips, "Cancer Coaching: Cardiology Coaching: Guide for Hope," Cancer Coaching | Cardiology Coaching | Guide for Hope, 2019, https://www.guideforhope.com/home.html.

CHAPTER 3

COMMON CANCER TERMINOLOGY YOUR DOCTOR MAY USE

Cancer is a disease that occurs from the uncontrolled growth of cells in our body. When these cells get out of control, they prevent our body from functioning normally.

Metastatic means that the cancer has spread from the original site to another place in the body. The most common sites cancer spreads to are the lymph nodes, bones, liver, lung, and brain. Where a cancer spreads to is often related to where the cancer started. Cancer that has spread to other parts of the body can be painful. While cancers that have metastasized are not curable, they are treatable.

Hematologic cancers are cancers that start within the blood or lymphatic system. Sometimes people think of these as bone cancer, but they are really cancer of the system that produces white blood cells, red blood cells, or platelets. These cancers are staged differently than solid tumors since our blood system is throughout our body.

Solid tumors are those cancers that start in an organ, such as the breast, colon, or lung.

White blood cells are our infection fighters. There are many types of white blood cells, each with its own job in helping our immune system. Chemotherapy and other cancer treatments can lower the number of white blood cells your body has available, making it difficult to fight off infections. Most doctors want you to call them if you have a fever of 100.4°F or higher, as this may be a sign of infection that would be difficult for your body to fight.

Red blood cells are the blood cells that carry oxygen throughout our body. When we have too few red blood cells, we are considered anemic. Chemotherapy and other cancer treatments may lower the number of red blood cells available. Call your doctor if you feel short of breath or very tired.

Platelets are cells that help to stop bleeding. When platelets are low from chemotherapy, you may notice you bruise easily.

Immune system is a system that is made up of a network of cells, tissues, and organs that work together to protect the body.

Hormones are substances that are produced in organs, circulate in the blood, and regulate both our behaviors and health. Hormones are normally produced in the human body and sometimes can be given in a medication to ensure enough of a hormone is present for the body to work properly. In breast and prostate cancers, medications are given to reduce the production of hormones that will allow the cancers to grow.

Stage of cancer / TNM stage. The stage of cancer is determined by the size of a tumor (T), how many lymph nodes (N) are involved in the local area, and how far outside the primary tumor the cancer has spread (M). Staging varies slightly by cancer type but generally follows a rule of stage 1 through stage 4.

Stage 1 cancers are small, with little to no lymph node involvement and have not spread beyond the first site of cancer. Stage 4 cancers tend to be larger, do involve lymph nodes, and have spread to sites beyond the first site of cancer. Many people relate stage 4 cancers to metastatic cancers and believe there is little that can be done for these individuals. While stage 4 cancers are metastatic and the prognosis is not as good as for those with stage 1 cancer, there are often many options for treating this cancer. Treatments do not provide a cure, but they can allow for a longer life and a better quality of life.

Chemotherapy is a single medication or group of medications used to treat a disease. In cancer care, we often think of chemotherapy as medication that is given by an intravenous (IV) line. Chemotherapy works by killing cells in a certain stage of their life. Unfortunately, this is also the type of treatment that causes several side effects, because it targets all cells at a certain stage of life.

Targeted therapy refers to medications that look for a specific marker in a cell and attach to that cell to kill it. This is very useful in tumors that have markers, such as VEGF, HER2neu, and others. These medications have different side effects than traditional chemotherapy. The side effects can include diarrhea, skin rashes, and low white blood cell counts.

Immunotherapy is a relatively new type of treatment for cancer. Immunotherapy works by supporting our own immune system. With some medications, the cancer cells are no longer able to hide, which allows our immune system to work naturally to kill cancer cells. Other medications teach our immune system to look for cancer cells, much like a vaccine teaches our immune system to look for viruses and bacteria, such as the flu or measles.

Genetic tests look for changes or mutations in the DNA or genes of an individual to see if there is an increased risk of developing cancer.

Tumor markers are anything present in or produced by cancer cells or other cells of the body in response to cancer that provides information about a cancer, such as how aggressive it is, whether it can be treated with a targeted therapy, or whether it is responding to treatment. Examples of tumor markers include ALK, BRAF, CEA, and CA19-9. A complete list of tumor markers can be found online at Cancer.Gov.[9]

---

[9] "Tumor Markers in Common Use," National Cancer Institute, last modified May 6, 2019, https://www.cancer.gov/about-cancer/diagnosis-staging/diagnosis/tumor-markers-list.

Complementary therapies are a group of diagnostic and therapeutic disciplines that are used together with conventional medicine. An example of a complementary therapy is using acupuncture in addition to usual care to help lessen a patient's discomfort following surgery.

Alternative medicine is any practice that aims to achieve the healing effects of medicine but that lacks biological plausibility and is untested, untestable, or proven ineffective.

Angiogenesis is the normal process responsible for the formation of new blood vessels from existing blood vessels. Tumors are able to hijack the normal process of new blood vessel growth for their own survival. Some cancer treatments target this process, preventing tumors from developing blood vessels that would provide the needed nutrition for the cancer to survive.

CHAPTER 4

KNOWING THE RIGHT QUESTIONS TO ASK

The January 2020 edition of the *American Society for Clinical Oncology—Connection* journal had a fabulous article to remind health care providers that sometimes it is more important to design a treatment plan that a patient can live with instead of insisting on the perfect treatment plan. The article suggested that both physicians and patients need to have open discussions. These discussions should include information about what chemotherapy is, how chemotherapy works, and/ or possible misconceptions about chemotherapy.

It is important to share with your doctor your experiences with cancer, both good and bad. We continue to learn about cancer and chemotherapy daily. There are new and exciting treatments approved and developed every day. Talk to your physician. Ask questions. Be open to understanding the opportunities that are available to you today and tomorrow. Remain positive and have *hope*. We know that in all things, God works for the good of those who love him, who have been called according to his purpose (Romans 8:28 NIV).

An article by Rae Nudson, "The Smartest Questions to Ask Your Doctor," gives the following advice: "It is absolutely appropriate to ask whatever question you need," says Martha Perry, a pediatrician at University of North Carolina and UNC Children's Hospital[10]. If a doctor responds unfavorably or doesn't answer a patient's question, she adds, that doctor isn't doing their job. Patients are often reluctant to ask questions as a result of self-consciousness or a lack of medical knowledge. If you want to be a more informed, proactive patient but aren't sure how to start, here are some questions to bring up at your next appointment.

- "What type of cancer do I have? Are there specific genetic traits or tumor markers this cancer has that I should know about? What is the stage of the cancer, including number of lymph nodes, if any, and sites of metastatic spread, if any?" If metastatic disease is present, asking about the extent of the metastatic disease

---

[10] Rae Nudson, "Elemental Medium," *Elemental Medium* (blog), March 2019, https://elemental.medium.com/the-smartest-questions-to-ask-your-doctor-b12757820524.

and the location can help in understanding your prognosis.

- A good follow-up question is "How concerned about this should I be?" This question allows a patient to get a clearer idea of how serious their cancer is.

- "What are the next steps to take? Do I need more tests? Is surgery appropriate? How and when are treatments given? Do I have options around treatment types? Why are you recommending the treatment you are?"

- Give doctors a green light to be more honest with you about what's happening by asking questions starting with "I know you don't have all the information yet, but what do you think will happen?" or by asking about the best- and worst-case scenarios.

- "Who will be managing my care? When should I call my primary care doctor, and when should I call my oncologist? Which doctor is making the decisions about my care?"

- "What is your general philosophy of care?" It's important to make sure your expectations and values line up with the way your doctor will be treating you. Ask questions about the use of complementary therapies and their views on alternative treatments.

- "What side effects or symptoms should I be looking for?"

- "How do you prefer that I communicate with you?" With the increased use of website patient portals and texting, doctors' offices are changing the way they communicate with patients.

- You should also ask how your doctor's office communicates test results. Some offices only share results if there is something wrong or abnormal, and others will get in touch no matter what. Knowing what your doctor's office does can keep you from anxiously waiting for a call that will never come.

- Say the weird thing on your mind—and say thank you.

You should always share your worries with your doctor, even if you think they seem silly. Voicing your concerns, no matter how unrealistic, can bring you peace of mind. "Doctors are very good about giving reassurance to patients if they know that they need it,[10]" Nathan Wood of Wayne State University says.

If you are worried that a doctor will judge you for asking questions, Perry suggests thanking them first. "A lot of times, [patients] just ask the questions and thank them afterwards. But if you preempt it with, 'I really appreciate you for answering my questions,' it sorts of put them in that position of having to answer," she says. "If the provider doesn't respond in a favorable way, then honestly I think that makes the provider look stupid.[10]"

CHAPTER 5

SHARING A CANCER DIAGNOSIS WITH LOVED ONES

Once you have learned you have cancer, a decision about sharing the news of your diagnosis becomes a task to be undertaken. You may find that you want to share with some individuals and not others. This is your choice to make. Do what is most comfortable for you. It is also OK for you to change your mind about discussing your diagnosis during your journey. You may even find that you want to share your diagnosis differently with different individuals, such as children or coworkers. So, how do you share a cancer diagnosis? When is the appropriate time, and what details do you share?

Sharing your diagnosis is not a simple conversation. It can be awkward and can become emotional. It is, however, a conversation most people have with at least their close family and friends. The best way to share is in person or over the phone, according to Dr. Ryan of Henry Ford Health System[11]. Sharing this news via email, text, or social media is not the best idea and could leave friends or family members in a state of panic and confusion. If you have a lot of people to tell, one way to get the news out is to designate a spokesperson—your caregiver or another close person in your life who can reach out to extended family and friends on your behalf.

Once family and friends have been informed of your

---

[11] Michael Ryan, "Henry Ford Health System," *Henry Ford Health System* (blog), February 2017, https://www.henryford.com/blog/2017/02/share-not-share-cancer-diagnosis.

diagnosis, sharing updates through social media can be a great way to keep everyone informed. This can also be a place for your support network to post thoughts of love and encouragement.

One of the issues many people face when sharing their cancer diagnosis is not wanting to feel like a burden—or feeling like they have to provide the emotional support to their loved ones who are struggling to cope with the diagnosis. "In order to reduce burden on you as the patient, it's important to communicate what your needs are," Dr. Ryan says. "If you have a family member who falls apart every time, he or she sees you, you need to be honest with that person. Say something like, 'I need you to be here for my emotional support, and if you can't, I need you to get the help you need.[11]'"

Cancer can be a tough disease to hide, especially during treatment. Coworkers, neighbors, and even people at the gym will most likely start to notice something is different and will probably be curious. In the end, it's up to you if you want to share. But telling those outside of your immediate circle could strengthen your support group and even add some external support to your caregivers.

In thinking about sharing the news about your cancer diagnosis, it can be helpful to plan how you would like to request help from those you speak with. One great place to start is meal planning. Diet and nutrition both during and after cancer therapy is an area where many individuals seek more information. A great resource is *Eating Well Through Cancer* by Holly Clegg. Each section offers insights into managing eating while dealing with the different side effects of treatment. The book also speaks to caregivers, answering questions such as "What can friends and family do to help?" Some suggestions include the following:

1. Offer encouragement and support without being overwhelming.

2. Offer to accompany a loved one with cancer to the grocery store.

3. Have a friend or loved one take your shopping list and go to the grocery store for you.

4. Organize friends/family who would like to cook for you and your family. *Take Them a Meal* is a good website to help with organizing things

5. Bring meals in disposable containers with paper plates and plasticware.

Some of the greatest opportunities to support loved ones with cancer will be in simple actions such as being present to listen, offering a warm smile, and providing a thoughtful snack or meal. I encourage you to share this information with loved ones. I often hear of family members who overwhelm individuals with cancer, as they feel a need to take over every part of the individual with cancer's life. This is not healthy for you or them. Remind them there will be times when you need to be alone to rest and recover, and there will be times when you need company and a shoulder to lean on. Most likely, you will not want or need a babysitter. It is OK for you to speak up and share that with those around you. There is a vast difference between supporting and hovering.

According to the American Cancer Society, it is helpful when friends and family members provide a comforting presence and practical support. However, it can be difficult for others to know what to say or how to start a conversation with someone who has cancer. Staying in touch is always better than staying away. Here are some tips to help you show your support:

- Take your cues from the person with cancer. Ask the person with cancer if they would like to talk about the experience. It is best to allow him or her to decide when to talk and how much to share.

- Show support without words. Your body and facial expressions can also convey your message of care and support. Keep eye contact, listen attentively, and avoid distractions when talking. One important way to provide support is to share some silence without needing to drown it out with chatter.

- Choose your words carefully. Make sure to acknowledge how difficult this experience is for the person. Carefully choosing what you say can help you show your support without being dismissive or avoiding the topic. For example, it is better to say, "I don't know what to say," than to stop calling or visiting out of fear.

Here are some things you can say to help show your care and support:

- I'm sorry this has happened to you.
- If you ever feel like talking, I'm here to listen.
- What are you thinking of doing, and how can I help?
- I care about you.
- I'm thinking about you.

Here are examples of phrases that are unhelpful:

- I know just how you feel.
- I know just what you should do.
- I know someone who had the exact same diagnosis.
- I'm sure you'll be fine.
- Don't worry.
- How long do you have?

Practice active listening. This is a technique that professionals use to show respect. It is a helpful way for you to show that you are connecting to the person's words and feelings. To be an active listener, give your full attention and avoid thinking about what to say next or hurrying the conversation and forcing it to a conclusion.

Use caution when asking questions. Phrase your questions carefully and consider the number of questions that you ask in a conversation. People with cancer are often asked many questions by their friends and family members, and it can become overwhelming.

Before you offer any advice, ask if it is OK and be prepared to stop if you are not encouraged to continue. If you feel the need to make a suggestion, ask for permission to share it first. Unsolicited advice may cause unnecessary stress.

Be honest about your feelings but do not overburden. Communicate feelings you may be experiencing—such as fear, anxiety, anger, or disbelief—in response to the person's cancer diagnosis. But try to be brief in your explanations. Spending too much time expressing difficult emotions you are feeling may overwhelm and upset the person with cancer. If you struggle to maintain your composure, give yourself some time away to calm your feelings before talking again. You may find that meeting with a counselor helps you process and manage your emotions.

Talk about topics other than cancer. Talking about everyday topics that you would normally discuss may help provide a sense of balance. The intent is not to distract your friend or family member but to help him or her maintain their interests and connections and to take a break from difficult conversations.

Encourage the individual with cancer to stay involved. Their involvement may look a bit different, but finding ways for them to be involved may provide a positive moment for them. Help them decide how to stay involved in their typical activities and continue old routines. Zoom access to group meetings has opened doors to stay involved that weren't available previously. Keep in mind a lack of time or energy from cancer or its treatment may prevent some people from usual activities and routines.

You may be able to help your friend or family member prioritize the activities they want to do and delegate other tasks. For example, you can suggest that your friend or family member saves energy to attend a child's soccer game or school play while asking for volunteers to help with household chores.

Ask if practical support would be helpful. Offer specific examples of ways you could help during cancer treatment. Ask if those suggestions sound helpful. Ideas include running errands, caring for pets, driving the person to an appointment, or picking up children from school. This approach is better than saying, "Let me know if you need any help," because some people have a hard time asking for help. If there are a lot of friends and family members volunteering to help, you may want to offer to coordinate everyone's efforts. CaringBridge is an example of an online community that provides tools to help manage everyone's involvement.

CHAPTER 6

CANCER AND FINDING A DIET THAT WORKS FOR YOU

Our diet is the main way our bodies obtain nutrients. These nutrients, such as vitamins and minerals, are important to our health and to healing. There is truth to sayings such as "You are what you eat." Diabetes, heart conditions, and even some immune disorders have been attributed to diet. According to the American Institute for Cancer Research, more than 120,000 cases of cancer each year are caused by obesity. Sixty-nine percent of

Americans are overweight (BMI 25+) or obese (BMI 30+). Forty percent of all cancers diagnosed in the US are related to obesity, lack of physical activity, excess alcohol consumption, and/or poor nutrition.

Good nutrition is important, whether you are trying to prevent cancer or trying to improve the outcomes of cancer treatment. The good news is that little changes make a big difference. For example, apples bind twenty times their weight; as a result, if everyone would eat just one small apple a day, up to thirty-six thousand new cancers a year in the US could be prevented. Another change that can be helpful is eliminating omega-6 fatty acids and increasing omega-3 fatty acids in the diet. Omega-6 fats tend to suppress the immune system, while omega-3 fats tend to boost the immune system. Omega-6 fats include soybean, corn, safflower, sunflower, "vegetable," and cottonseed oils. Eliminating these fats will strengthen your immune system. Eliminating omega-6 fats may also help prevent Parkinson's and Alzheimer's diseases. Sources of omega-3 include wild cold-water fish like salmon, sardines, and anchovies; grass-fed beef; wild game; pastured hens and their eggs; raw walnuts, pumpkin, flax, hemp, and chia seeds.

Eating five to nine servings of fruits and veggies each day can be easy. Serving sizes are small: one medium fruit, a half cup of broccoli, or one cup of salad. Think outside the box to eat more of the *green stuff*. Some of these suggestions may be helpful for any of us who shy away from green things on our plate.

Try these ideas:

1. Shred carrots or zucchini into meatloaf, burgers, and casseroles. Place chopped vegetables in pasta sauce, lasagna, soups, chili, and mashed potatoes.

2. Put lettuce or slices of cucumber, tomato, green pepper, or roasted red pepper in a sandwich for lunch. Or add a side of baby carrots.

3. Try snacks of chopped veggies with a low-fat dressing or dip.

4. Cook a vegetable stir-fry.

5. Cook fish, chicken, lean beef, or pork tenderloin with vegetables to add flavor, color, and nutrition at mealtime.

6. Add a supplement, such as Juice Plus. Your body will begin to crave fruits and vegetables as a result. More information on Juice Plus can be found online.

7. And above all, *keep trying.*

Hungry for Health by Susan Silberstein, PhD, is a wonderful resource for recipes that help prevent cancer. If you already have a diagnosis of cancer, her recipes and suggestions will help strengthen your immune system and begin the healing process so you can achieve long-term success. This book and others can be purchased by going to BeatCancer.org

Other books that contain healthy recipes include the following:

- *A Cancer Battle Plan* by Anne E. Frahm and David J Frahm
- *The Whole Food Guide for Breast Cancer Survivors* by Edward Bauman and Helayne Waldman
- *Betty Crocker Living with Cancer Cookbook* by Betty Crocker Cooking
- The American Cancer Society's *Healthy Eating Cookbook: A Celebration of Food, Friendship, and Healthy Living*

- *What to Eat if You Have Cancer (Revised): Healing Foods That Boost Your Immune System* by Maureen Keane and Daniella Chace
- *The Cancer-Fighting Kitchen* by Rebecca Katz

Sugar is another dietary product that there is a lot of confusion around. Sugar is in all our foods, and our body needs glucose to create energy. We don't need to eliminate all sugar; we need to be cautious of large amounts of sugar. Research shows that it is sugar's relationship to higher insulin levels and related growth factors that may influence cancer cell growth the most and increase the risk of other chronic diseases. Some cancer cells have insulin receptors, which makes them respond more than normal cells to insulin's ability to promote growth. Sugar has also been shown to suppress our immune system for up to five hours after eating large amounts. By selecting foods that are as close to the way they were when they came out of the ground, you can avoid a significant amount of added sugar in your diet.

Client testimony. Almost ten months ago, I met to discuss what could be done to help her heal her body from a precancerous lesion. We met briefly each month to discuss diet and exercise. At first, her diet was based on red meat and carbs. She exercised occasionally but was "busy with life." Each month, she made little changes. She added Juice Plus capsules at first. "At least it is some fruits and vegetables." She slowly began adding real fruits and vegetables. She added in flaxseed oil and spirulina to ensure her immune system was at its strongest. She began exercising and even ran a half-marathon. Today, she called with great news: the precancerous lesion was gone! In its place was a mild infection that would be treated with an inexpensive antibiotic. No surgery, no missing weeks of work, and no long recovery. She was ecstatic!

CHAPTER 7

CANCER AND CHOOSING COMPLEMENTARY PRACTICES

While diet is certainly an important part of healing, there are other things you can do to strengthen your body and improve the odds for living a vibrant life with cancer. This next chapter will highlight many of the practices that are safe to incorporate into your care and will help you feel better. As always, it is a good idea to discuss anything you decide to add to your care with your health care provider.

Prayer is often seen as an activity for those who are religious. And maybe it is. What I can tell you is that prayer works, especially when we ask for God's will to be done. I have seen miracles occur when people pray and are prayed for. My best friend's mom was diagnosed with metastatic endometrial cancer and was quite ill. Her church prayed, she was added to prayer lists across the globe, her family prayed, and she prayed. Her first chemotherapy treatment resulted in severe side effects that resulted in her staying in the intensive care unit for weeks. No one knew if she would pull through, but everyone continued to pray for a miracle. Fifteen years later, my friend's mom is cancer-free and doing amazingly well. She never required another round of chemotherapy. Miracles do happen. God may not answer every prayer the way we want, but we can know that He is faithful.

Jeremiah 29:11 says, "'For I know the plans I have for you,' declares the LORD, 'plans to prosper you and not to harm you, plans to give you hope and a future.'"

If you are unfamiliar with prayer, a good place to start is just speaking out loud your thoughts. Another option is reading the Psalms. The Psalms are the prayers of King David and King Solomon at different junctures of their lives. Some give praise, and some ask for forgiveness or strengthen in a difficult time. Reading these passages can provide a sense of peace, as you can see God's hand on all of life's ups and downs. God will never forget the needy; the hope of the afflicted will never perish (Psalm 9:18 NIV).

Faith is a large part of prayer. Faith is believing that someone larger than us can intervene and take away our suffering. As a believer in Christ, my faith drives the way I care for and pray for patients. It is also why I include here an opportunity to know a God so strong and mighty that he can take away pain and even heal an individual with cancer. Does God always take away our sufferings? Of course not. But he is always willing to give us strength to deal with what we are going through. The Bible talks about needing to have faith as big as a mustard seed to move mountains. "Truly I tell you, if you have faith as small as a mustard seed, you can say to this mountain, 'Move from here to there,' and it will move. Nothing will be impossible for you" (Matthew 17:20 NIV). That's not much faith, but the results are undeniable. Faith not only helps individuals deal with their circumstances, but it encourages those supporting them.

John 3:16 (NIV) states, "For God so loved the world that he gave his one and only Son, that whoever believes in him shall not perish but have eternal life." God loves you, and that love came in the human form of Jesus. A prayer for salvation sounds something like this: "Salvation is a gift that only God can give. Right now, I place my faith in Jesus Christ as God's Son who died for my sins and rose from the dead to give me eternal life. Please forgive me of my sins and help me to live for you. Thank you for accepting me and giving me eternal life." If you prayed that prayer, we would love to support you in strengthening your faith. Reach out to us at info@ guideforhope.com.

Meditation is a practice where an individual uses mindfulness to improve attention and awareness, allowing them to achieve a mentally clear or emotionally calm and stable state. In easier to understand terms, meditation is a way to calm and quiet your mind so that you can think clearly. Meditation is best done in a quiet place where you will not be distracted. When beginning a meditation program, give yourself time to learn to quiet your mind. Start meditating in five- or ten-minute increments. You can build up to longer amounts of time when you are ready.

Studies have shown that cancer patients who try to visualize their body attacking their cancer while meditating have an increase in the effectiveness of their treatments. Visualization is a type of meditation where you place yourself in the future, accomplishing goals you have set and overcoming your cancer. Your doctor's office may have meditation tapes they can lend you. Omvana is one app that guides you through visualization and meditation scripts as you learn to meditate on your own. It is an easy way to get started meditating and reap the benefits of relaxation. The cancer coaches at Guide for Hope can also walk you through some guided meditations if you feel you need extra support.

Mindfulness is the ability to keep the mind focused on the present moment. In a clinical study completed at Fox Chase Cancer Center in Philadelphia, Pennsylvania, mindfulness was associated with less pain, fatigue, anxiety, depression, and sleep disturbance in women with metastatic breast cancer. Lauren A. Zimmaro, PhD, postdoctoral fellow of the Cancer Prevention and Control Program at Fox Chase Cancer Center, says, "Not judging or reacting to symptoms may be helpful to the physical body by lowering the fight-or-flight stress response and inducing a relaxation response. Over time, people who are more mindful can buffer their stresses, and that may have a more beneficial impact on the body.[12]"

Reiki is a form of alternative medicine called energy healing that was developed by a Japanese Buddhist monk in the early twentieth century. Reiki practitioners use a technique called palm healing or hands-on healing through which a universal energy is said to be transferred through the palms of the practitioner to the patient in order to encourage emotional or physical healing and to promote a sense of well-being. Reiki has been found to

[12] Lauren Zimmaro, "Fox Chase Cancer Center," *Fox Chase Cancer Center* (blog), *Temple Health*, November 8, 2019.

reduce anxiety and pain, which may improve quality of life. Interestingly, advanced reiki can also be performed remotely. Many cancer centers have Reiki practitioners on staff that they can refer you to. All individuals, regardless of their diagnosis, can take advantage of the benefits of Reiki.

Exercise is another great practice you can undertake to live well with cancer. Exercise has been shown to be beneficial to all cancer patients and helps reduce fatigue and weight gain. *JAMA Network* published an article that highlights the importance of weight training as part of an exercise program for individuals with cancer[13]. Weight training improves bone density, reduces fat tissue, and improves insulin sensitivity and glucose levels—all important to improving cancer outcomes. Why not try lifting some light weights while watching TV? Exercise

---

[13] Kathryn H. Schmitz et al., "Weight Lifting for Women at Risk for Breast Cancer–Related Lymphedema," *JAMA* 304, no. 24 (December 2010): 2699, https://doi.org/10.1001/jama.2010.1837.

can be as simple as walking to the mailbox or as complex as going to the gym. Start slowly, but make sure to start.

Aromatherapy is the practice of using the fragrances from plants to promote physical and psychological well-being. Fragrances that can help with anxiety and depression include bergamot, cedarwood (atlas), and chamomile, among many others. Essential oils can be used topically or through breathing in the fragrance by using diffusers or nebulizers. Even fragrant teas can provide some of the benefits of aromatherapy. If you are looking for an easy way to relax, aromatherapy may be the right choice.

Acupuncture is a form of Traditional Chinese Medicine that has been around for approximately 2,500 years. It is considered a type of alternative medicine in the US. The theory behind acupuncture is that there are specific patterns of energy flow that are required for good health. Disease or illness occurs when these energy patterns are blocked or altered in some way. Throughout Asia, acupuncture is performed slightly differently. Acupuncturists use a special technique to insert thin needles into the skin at specific locations. These thin needles are then manipulated by the provider or by using electrical stimulation.

Clinical studies of acupuncture have shown a potential benefit for reducing nausea, vomiting, pain, and neuropathy. Acupuncture offers an alternative to narcotic pain medications, with limited side effects. Side effects may include bleeding at the needle insertion site, bruising, pain, or sometimes dizziness. Severe adverse effects are rare but may include infection or pneumothorax. It is important that if you are considering acupuncture, you use a qualified provider.

Journaling is a fabulous complement to your treatments and one I highly recommend. It can reduce stress, help you gain clarity, help you make decisions, and even help you regulate your emotions. All of these are important on your cancer journey. How or what should be written in a journal is a question I am often asked. Some people recommend writing just for a few minutes about whatever is on your mind. This could be a few sentences or a few paragraphs. I recommend writing down questions and thoughts you have about your diagnosis, treatment, and side effects. Keeping a record of your thoughts and how you are feeling each day can help your health care team better understand how you are responding to treatment. Share your journal with them, even those pieces of information that may feel uncomfortable to share. There are many ways your health care team can help if they know what you are experiencing.

Other things that are helpful to journal about include things you have learned and things you are thankful for. Writing down things you have learned about your treatment or diagnosis will help you remember the information longer. It can also be a place to write down those things you have learned about yourself, such as an inner strength you only recently recognized. Journaling creates a history of your life. No matter where you are in your life journey, having a history to share with loved ones can strengthen bonds and create close ties. Individuals who utilize Guide for Hope's cancer-coaching services receive a free journal as part of the program.

Having the right mindset is crucial to beating cancer. Affirmations can help you stay positive and allow you to visualize cancer leaving your body. According to the law of natural attraction, affirmations are positive sentences that you repeat to yourself to build up self-belief in the subconscious mind. The top benefits of daily affirmations include the following:

- You can boost your problem-solving skills by using self-affirmation. So, affirmations can help you make decisions about your care.

- Affirmations make you more aware of your thought processes. Greater awareness makes you more likely to challenge negative thoughts as they arise. This also enhances your self-knowledge, making you better at knowing what you really want.

- Positive affirmations reconnect you with feelings of gratitude and enhance your perspective on the good things in life. This can boost your happiness.

Most people are not used to incorporating affirmations into their day. How to do this is easy and straightforward. Start by writing down sentences about what you would like to see happen. Read these sentences out loud once a day or multiple times a day. You can also write them out on a daily basis. Using multiple senses to make these affirmations come alive will increase the impact they will have.

Here are some examples of affirmations for cancer patients:

- Cancer is something I can go through. It does not define me; it is just an experience in my life.

- My body is learning to find and remove cancer cells from my body.

- I heal with every inhalation and let go of cancer with every exhalation.

- Miracles happen every day, and cancer is not immune to their magic. I choose miracles.

For additional affirmations, visit www.freeaffirmations. org/survive-cancer-positive-affirmations.

Music is another great way to create a positive environment. "Hold on," you may say. "Listening to sad songs is what we do when we are going through difficult experiences. How does that create a positive environment?" Listening to uplifting music is a better solution. Find songs that are positive and encouraging and lift your spirits instead of those that focus on difficult situations. A few examples follow:

- Mandisa, "Overcomer"
- Kelly Clarkson, "Stronger"
- Unspoken, "Reason"
- Gloria Gaynor, "I will Survive"
- Bobby McFerrin, "Don't Worry Be Happy"

Did you know there is a scientific name for the study of laughter? Gelotology is really the study of laughter and its effects on the body. So, what do these scientists of laughter tell us? They say laughter is good for us. Laughter increases the production of hormones that help us feel good and reduces the production of stress hormones. Laughter can lower blood pressure, provide exercise, and improve our immune system so we can naturally fight infection and cancer.

Sometimes it may be difficult to laugh. Dealing with cancer doesn't normally provide opportunities to find something to laugh about. How can we incorporate more laughter into our lives? Here are some suggestions:

- Watch a funny video.
- Call a friend with a good sense of humor.
- Wander the greeting card aisle and find a few cards that make you giggle. No purchase required.
- Start a gratitude journal or a memory board so that you can go back to and look at the things that have made you smile or laugh.

- Spend a few minutes talking to a child. They really do say the funniest things, and you never know what they will say next.
- Try laugh yoga. Yes, it is a real thing. Go to www.laughteryoga.org. You can't help but laugh just watching …

CHAPTER 8

CANCER AND FILTERING ADVICE

Recently, the American Society of Oncology (ASCO) published an article that highlights some of the important things that all of us should be watching for. It may be helpful to ask yourself some questions when considering advice given by anyone outside of your health care team.

1. Is the advice improving my relationship with my physician?

2. Is the advice helping me to become more empowered?

3. Do I feel better supported in my journey?

4. Am I able to find information that relates to my situation so that I can better care for myself?

5. Have I been able to find a clinical trial or other research related to my care?

If you can answer these questions in a positive manner, then you are on the right track!

However, there are some other questions that still need to be asked, such as these:

1. Should I be talking to my health care team about this question or concern?

2. Am I confident the information shared is from a quality source?

3. Is the source claiming a cure using unproven methods?

4. Are they providing too much information, causing confusion?

5. Are they protecting my privacy?

The answer to these questions should also guide your decision about moving forward with any advice given by anyone other than your health care team.

CHAPTER 9

CANCER AND UNDERSTANDING THE FINANCIAL IMPACT

After figuring out the details about their cancer and even exploring some information on what they can do to help improve their outcomes, many individuals find themselves asking the question "How do I pay for this?" *Financial toxicity* is a relatively new term that is often heard in cancer clinics. It refers to the cost of treatment that goes above and beyond just the cost of the surgery, chemotherapy, or radiation. It is meant to raise awareness of the costs of treatment that may mean a family or individual needs to choose between buying medications and keeping the electric bill paid. Cancer patients are 2.65 times more likely to declare bankruptcy than those without cancer, and those who file for bankruptcy have a 79 percent greater risk of early mortality[14]. Sharing any financial challenges with your health care team is essential to prevent financial toxicity and an important part of the healing process.

When thinking about the cost of cancer, it is important to think beyond the cost of treatment. The cost of treatment is a big factor, and understanding what your insurance will and will not pay for is important. But don't stop there. Think about the unseen costs that you may incur, such as these:

[14] Carla Tardiff, "What Is CRFT? • Family Reach," Family Reach, February 27, 2020, https://familyreach.org/crft/.

- taking time off work, for both you and your spouse
- hiring someone to help around the house
- childcare
- transportation to and from appointments
- meals away from home as a result of appointments
- hotel costs if your treatments are far from home

Make sure to keep receipts, as you may be able to request a tax credit for these and other medical expenses that you incur.

So, now that you have a general idea of what it will cost for your care, how can you make it affordable? Step one: don't panic. Here are some ideas of places to start:

- Talk with the financial office at the cancer clinic to get a better understanding of what your insurance will pay for and the options available for paying any out-of-pocket expenses.

- Create a budget using the information gathered.

- Consult with a financial planner. They may be willing to provide free services if you let them know you have been diagnosed with cancer.

- Talk with the social worker at the cancer center. Often, they can help guide you to appropriate options, such as co-pay cards and cost-savings programs.

- Did you know there is a government program to help with student loan debt for cancer patients? Contact your student loan company if you are undergoing active treatment; they should be willing and able to help.

- Family Reach is a nonprofit organization that provides financial counseling and financial support for families facing cancer. They have a number of online resources that can help identify areas of need early so you can get the help needed.

- Create a fundraising page. This is a great way to involve friends and family who are creative and outgoing.

- Cancer + Careers is an organization that advocates for cancer survivors in the workplace, providing information and tools for providers and patients about working during and/or after treatment for cancer. A checklist is provided on the website, and it lists questions to help you talk to your doctor about any potential issues or concerns you may have about working. Cancer + Careers also provides some suggestions for patients to help cope with the effects of cancer or its treatment while at work, including tips to fight fatigue, nausea, gastrointestinal issues, mucositis, and techniques to maintain a positive attitude. The website also provides a link to the National Coalition for Cancer Survivorship (NCCS) publication about employment rights as a cancer survivor, which describes the legal rights of patients and employers.

CHAPTER 10

CANCER AND MORE RESOURCES AVAILABLE TO YOU

Having resources to guide your journey can also be helpful. Some of my favorite resources are highlighted in this chapter. Take control of your health by using these resources to be better informed. There is power in knowledge.

An older book but one that provides inspiration from the perspective of a pastor who developed cancer is *Coping with Cancer* by John Packo. In his book, Pastor

Packo explains the twelve choices he made to help him live with his cancer and for God. There are Creative Choice cards at the end of the book that tie together the Bible verses supporting that choice.

Radical Remission—Surviving Cancer Against All Odds is a book written by Kelly A. Turner, PhD. Her book is based on research of patients who have defied the odds and survived serious cancer diagnoses. She highlights nine key factors that these patients shared and which she believes made the difference in their outcome. These include the following:

- change in diet
- taking control of your health
- following your intuition
- using herbs and supplements
- letting go of suppressed emotions
- increasing positive emotions

- embracing social support
- deepening your spiritual connection
- having a strong reason for living

I recommend that you read the book for yourself. Not every recommendation in Dr. Turner's book will be right for every patient. Speak to your health care team prior to making any of the above changes. Communication will ensure the best possible outcome.

Blue Zones by Dan Buettner is another excellent book that highlights research done on the lifestyles of some of the world's longest-living individuals. The book also includes recipes for living longer that are plant based. It encourages getting involved in the community to find purpose. Some suggestions include attending religious services and volunteering. Other suggestions follow:

- getting natural exercise through walking, gardening, and manual chores instead of using electronics

- spending time with family, especially at meals
- eating a larger meal in the morning or early afternoon
- eating evening meals that are smaller and with a glass of red wine
- limiting sweets to special occasions

Cancer Hates Tea by Maria Uspenski is a very interesting book, especially if you like tea. There are recipes for incorporating tea into your diet and information on how tea enhances your immune system.

Frankly Speaking about Cancer are webinars that offer patients and their family educational resources on living with cancer. Leaders in oncology discuss the latest medical information in an easy-to-understand format to empower patients and their families to make informed decisions about their cancer care. Webinars include topics such as these:

- living with cancer
- managing side effects
- cancer types
- clinical trials
- caregivers
- immunotherapy

There are many opportunities to learn more about your specific cancer as well as ways to become empowered through your journey. Take time to seek out the information you need to make an informed decision. Journal and reflect on the successes you have achieved; you will be surprised at how many there are. Most of all, be encouraged. "Have I not commanded you? Be strong and courageous. Do not be afraid; do not be discouraged, for the LORD your God will be with you wherever you go" (Joshua 1:9).

CHAPTER 11

CONCLUSION

The goal of this book is quite broad. The first and most important goal is to empower individuals diagnosed with cancer to successfully navigate the journey ahead. Guide for Hope believes that through a strong faith in God and information to make informed decisions, a life with cancer can be a joyous, memorable, and successful experience. Everyone will need to determine what success is for them as they follow the path before them. No two people will have the same experience on this path. It is important not to compare yourself to others. Follow your heart when making decisions, knowing that you know yourself better than anyone else does.

There are many opportunities for support and empowerment, as we have outlined within the pages of this book. Take advantage of the chapter focused on loved ones and use the ideas to obtain the support you need. Learn more about nutrition and how it can impact your immune system. The complementary therapies mentioned can reduce anxiety and provide much-needed rest. We encourage you to "Look to the Lord and his strength; seek his face always" (1 Chronicles 16:11). Your faith will not only help you through this time, but it will also allow you to be a testimony to those around you. Stay strong and know that we are praying for God to perform his will in your life.

The second goal is to give back and promote cancer research. A percentage of the proceeds from this book will be given to cancer charities, such as the American

Cancer Society, Leukemia and Lymphoma Society, and Family Reach. Each year, five charities will be chosen to be the recipients of the proceeds. Recommendations for worthy charities that are improving the lives of individuals with cancer can be shared with us at <u>info@ guideforhope.com.</u>

"What Cancer Cannot Do"
(author unknown)

Cancer is so limited
It cannot cripple love,
shatter hope,
kill friendship,
erode the spirit,
take away faith,
silence courage,
destroy peace,
suppress memories,
or conquer the soul.

ABOUT GUIDE FOR HOPE AND THE AUTHOR

Guide for Hope began organically as friends and family reached out to Ruth for her support and advice after being diagnosed with cancer. As a licensed registered nurse in Pennsylvania with more than twenty-five years of clinical experience in oncology, Ruth was able to take her passion for helping cancer patients and extend it from the clinical environment to supporting individuals at home. Ruth offers a guiding hand to help answer questions with support options reflective of your individual diagnosis. *Hope for Your Cancer Journey* was written to support individuals diagnosed with cancer who are looking for guidance as they begin their cancer journey.

Client Testimonials

In February of 2018, I was diagnosed with colon cancer. I connected with Ruth through a friend. I had multitudes of unanswered questions. Because of her 25 years of knowledge, she was able to calm my fears and enabled me to move forward with my treatment. To me, she was a shelter in a storm. (Anonymous)

Speaking directly with a very experienced Oncology Nurse is like finding a beacon of hope in a time of need. Ruth's vast Oncology intelligence and experience hits every single mark. It's Ruth's generous and graceful manner that literally make for "A Guide for Hope." Everyone I have sent to her thanks ME for my help sending them to her. Don't wait. Call her now, she can undoubtedly help you. (Michelle from New York)

BIBLIOGRAPHY

Basch, Ethan, Allison M. Deal, Mark G. Kris, Howard I. Scher, Clifford A. Hudis, Paul Sabbatini, Lauren Rogak, et al. "Symptom Monitoring With Patient-Reported Outcomes During Routine Cancer Treatment: A Randomized Controlled Trial." *Journal of Clinical Oncology* 34, no. 6 (February 2016): 557–65. https://doi.org/10.1200/jco.2015.63.0830.

Connors, Andrea. "Digital Sherpa™ Program." Patient Empowerment Network, July 23, 2020. https://powerfulpatients.org/digital-sherpa-program/.

DelSole, Mona (blog). "Alex Trebec's Courageous Leadership." November 9, 2020. https://www.linkedin.com/pulse/alex-trebecs-courageous-leadership-mona-delsole-mpa/.

Duckworth, Angela. *Grit*. London: Vermilion, 2019.

Gleckman, Howard. "Big Strides in Cancer Treatment Will Increase Long-Term Care Needs." *Forbes*, June 10, 2015. https://www.forbes.com/sites/howardgleckman/2015/06/10/big-strides-in-cancer-treatment-will-increase-long-term-care-needs/?sh=d85050c627be.

Li, William W. "Keynote Presentation: Dietary Modification of the Tumor Microenvironment." Quoted "Angiogenesis and Nutritional Oncology: New Frontiers in the Approach to Cancer Therapy." *CCA News* 1, no. 2 (October 2020).

Nudson, Rae (blog). "The Smartest Questions to Ask Your Doctor." Web log. *Elemental Medium*, March 2019. https://elemental.medium.com/the-smartest-questions-to-ask-your-doctor-b12757820524.

Pande, Reena, Michael Morris, Aimee Peters, Claire Spettell, Richard Feifer, and William Gillis. "Leveraging Remote Behavioral Health Interventions to Improve Medical Outcomes and Reduce Costs." *The American Journal of Managed Care* 21, no. 2 (February 2015).

Phillips, Ruth. "Cancer Coaching: Cardiology Coaching: Guide for Hope." Cancer Coaching | Cardiology Coaching | Guide for Hope, 2019. https://www.guideforhope.com/home.html.

Ryan, Michael (blog). "How To Share (Or Not Share) A Cancer Diagnosis." Web log. *Henry Ford Health System*, February 2017. https://www.henryford.com/blog/2017/02/ share-not-share-cancer-diagnosis.

Schmitz, Kathryn H., Rehana L. Ahmed, Andrea B. Troxel, Andrea Cheville, Lorita Lewis-Grant, Rebecca Smith, Cathy J. Bryan, Catherine T. Williams-Smith, and Jesse Chittams. "Weight Lifting for Women at Risk for Breast Cancer–Related Lymphedema." *JAMA* 304, no. 24 (December 2010): 2699. https://doi.org/10.1001/ jama.2010.1837.

Tardiff, Carla. "What Is CRFT? • Family Reach." Family Reach, February 27, 2020. https://familyreach. org/crft/.

"Tumor Markers in Common Use." National Cancer Institute. Last modified May 6, 2019. https:// www.cancer.gov/about-cancer/diagnosis-staging/ diagnosis/tumor-markers-list.

Zimmaro, Lauren (blog). "Mindfulness May Help Women Cope With Metastatic Breast Cancer." Web log. *Fox Chase Cancer Center*. Temple Health, November 8, 2019.

04090048-00836282

Printed in the United States
by Baker & Taylor Publisher Services